ZIPPY READS

by Carla Golembe

ABCDEFGHIJKLM

For Jody Jaffe and John Muncie

NOPQRSTUVWXYZ

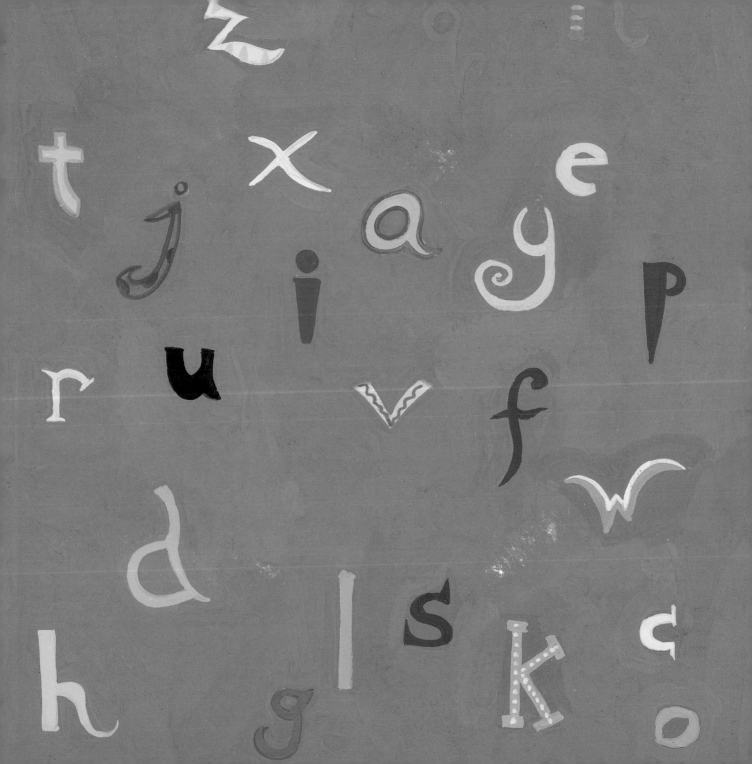

Zippy is a clever cat! He is learning how to read.

One morning Zippy says to Zoe, "Let's go for a walk.
I want to show you all the things I can read."

Zippy and Zoe walk down the street.

They see a store with letters on the roof.
"What does that say?" asks Zoe.

"B-A-N-K," Zippy reads. "Bank. It is where people save their money."

Zippy and Zoe walk some more.

They see a large *building.

*為生字，請參照生字表

"What do the letters above the door say?" asks Zoe.

"E-L-E-M-E-N-T-A-R-Y S-C-H-O-O-L," Zippy reads. "Elementary school. It is where children learn to read and write."

"They learn math and music and art, too," Zoe tells him.

Up the road Zoe sees a shop with roses in the window.
"What does that say?" she asks.
"F-L-O-W-E-R S-H-O-P," Zippy reads. "Flower shop."

"I love flowers," says Zoe.

Something smells good at the store next door.

"R-E-S-T-A-U-R-A-N-T," Zippy reads and his tummy makes a
loud noise. "Restaurant.

Oh, I want some pizza."

"I want some chocolate ice cream," Zoe says.

Zippy and Zoe walk by a house. They see a *sign in the garden.

"What does that say?" Zoe asks.

"D-A-N-G-E-R. K-E-E-P O-U-T. D-O-G!" Zippy reads. "That says danger, *keep out...."

But before he can finish, Zippy and Zoe hear a loud bark.
An angry dog is running *across the grass.

Zippy *yells, "DOG!!!!"

Zippy and Zoe run *as fast as they can. The dog runs behind them. They run past the restaurant,

the flower shop,

the elementary school and the bank.

They run to Zoe's house and close the door.
Zippy says, "Maybe I'll just read you a story at home."

生字表

n.＝名詞，prep.＝介系詞，v.＝動詞

賽ㄙㄞ皮ㄆㄧ學ㄒㄩㄝ認ㄖㄣ字ㄗ

🍕 *p.3*

賽ㄙㄞ皮ㄆㄧ是ㄕ一ㄧ隻ㄓ很ㄏㄣ聰ㄘㄨㄥ明ㄇㄧㄥ的ㄉㄜ貓ㄇㄠ，他ㄊㄚ正ㄓㄥ在ㄗㄞ學ㄒㄩㄝ認ㄖㄣ字ㄗ。

🍦 *p.4*

有ㄧㄡ一ㄧ天ㄊㄧㄢ早ㄗㄠ上ㄕㄤ，賽ㄙㄞ皮ㄆㄧ對ㄉㄨㄟ柔ㄖㄡ依ㄧ說ㄕㄨㄛ：「我ㄨㄛ們ㄇㄣ一ㄧ起ㄑㄧ去ㄑㄩ散ㄙㄢ步ㄅㄨ吧ㄅㄚ！我ㄨㄛ想ㄒㄧㄤ讓ㄖㄤ你ㄋㄧ看ㄎㄢ看ㄎㄢ我ㄨㄛ會ㄏㄨㄟ唸ㄋㄧㄢ哪ㄋㄚ些ㄒㄧㄝ字ㄗ。」

🍕 *p.5*

賽ㄙㄞ皮ㄆㄧ和ㄏㄜ柔ㄖㄡ依ㄧ沿ㄧㄢ著ㄓㄜ街ㄐㄧㄝ道ㄉㄠ走ㄗㄡ。

🍦 *p.6*

他ㄊㄚ們ㄇㄣ看ㄎㄢ到ㄉㄠ有ㄧㄡ家ㄐㄧㄚ店ㄉㄧㄢ的ㄉㄜ屋ㄨ頂ㄉㄧㄥ上ㄕㄤ有ㄧㄡ字ㄗ。
柔ㄖㄡ依ㄧ問ㄨㄣ：「上ㄕㄤ面ㄇㄧㄢ寫ㄒㄧㄝ了ㄌㄜ什ㄕㄣ麼ㄇㄜ呢ㄋㄜ？」

🍕 *p.7*

賽ㄙㄞ皮ㄆㄧ唸ㄋㄧㄢ著ㄓㄜ：「B-A-N-K，銀ㄧㄣ行ㄏㄤ。那ㄋㄚ是ㄕ大ㄉㄚ家ㄐㄧㄚ存ㄘㄨㄣ錢ㄑㄧㄢ的ㄉㄜ地ㄉㄧ方ㄈㄤ。」

p.8
賽皮和柔依再往前走。

p.9
他們看到一棟很大的建築物。

p.10
柔依問：「大門上方那排字是什麼意思呢？」

p.11
賽皮唸著：「E-L-E-M-E-N-T-A-R-Y S-C-H-O-O-L，小學。那是小朋友學習讀書和寫字的地方。」
柔依告訴他：「他們也會學數學、音樂和美術喔。」

p.12
在路上，柔依看到有一家店的櫥窗裡擺著玫瑰。
柔依問：「那些字又是什麼意思呢？」
賽皮唸著：「F-L-O-W-E-R S-H-O-P，花店。」

p.13
柔依說：「我喜歡花。」

p.14

隔壁的店裡傳來一陣香味。

賽皮唸著:「R-E-S-T-A-U-R-A-N-T。」他的肚子發出好大的叫聲。「是餐廳。」

p.15

「喔,我好想吃點披薩。」

柔依說:「我想吃巧克力冰淇淋。」

p.16

賽皮和柔依經過一間房子。他們看到庭院裡有個標語。

柔依問:「上面寫了什麼啊?」

p.17

賽皮唸著:「D-A-N-G-E-R。K-E-E-P O-U-T。D-O-G!它說:『危險,禁止進入……』」

p.18

但是賽皮的話還沒說完,他們就聽到好大的狗叫聲。有隻生氣的狗正越過草坪跑過來!

p.19

賽皮大叫：「內有惡犬！」

p.20

賽皮和柔依盡全力的逃跑，而那隻狗就在後面追著他們。他們跑過餐廳、

p.21

跑過花店、

p.22

跑過小學和銀行。

p.23

他們跑回柔依的家，然後把門關上。
賽皮說：「也許，我在家裡唸故事給你聽就好了。」

猜ㄘㄞ猜ㄘㄞ這ㄓㄜˋ是ㄕˋ哪ㄋㄚˇ裡ㄌㄧˇ？

Part. 1

　　小ㄒㄧㄠˇ朋ㄆㄥˊ友ㄧㄡˇ，故ㄍㄨˋ事ㄕˋ裡ㄌㄧˇ的ㄉㄜ賽ㄙㄞˋ皮ㄆㄧˊ帶ㄉㄞˋ著ㄓㄜ柔ㄖㄡˊ依ㄧ認ㄖㄣˋ識ㄕˋ了ㄌㄜ好ㄏㄠˇ多ㄉㄨㄛ英ㄧㄥ文ㄨㄣˊ單ㄉㄢ字ㄗˋ喔ㄛ！你ㄋㄧˇ是ㄕˋ不ㄅㄨˋ是ㄕˋ也ㄧㄝˇ已ㄧˇ經ㄐㄧㄥ學ㄒㄩㄝˊ會ㄏㄨㄟˋ這ㄓㄜˋ些ㄒㄧㄝ單ㄉㄢ字ㄗˋ了ㄌㄜ呢ㄋㄜ？一ㄧˋ起ㄑㄧˇ來ㄌㄞˊ做ㄗㄨㄛˋ下ㄒㄧㄚˋ面ㄇㄧㄢˋ的ㄉㄜ練ㄌㄧㄢˋ習ㄒㄧ，測ㄘㄜˋ試ㄕˋ一ㄧˊ下ㄒㄧㄚˋ自ㄗˋ己ㄐㄧˇ學ㄒㄩㄝˊ會ㄏㄨㄟˋ了ㄌㄜ多ㄉㄨㄛ少ㄕㄠˇ吧ㄅㄚ！請ㄑㄧㄥˇ看ㄎㄢˋ圖ㄊㄨˊ猜ㄘㄞ出ㄔㄨ這ㄓㄜˋ些ㄒㄧㄝ是ㄕˋ什ㄕㄣˊ麼ㄇㄜ地ㄉㄧˋ方ㄈㄤ，並ㄅㄧㄥˋ用ㄩㄥˋ英ㄧㄥ文ㄨㄣˊ拼ㄆㄧㄣ出ㄔㄨ來ㄌㄞˊ。

（正ㄓㄥˋ確ㄑㄩㄝˋ答ㄉㄚˊ案ㄢˋ在ㄗㄞˋ第ㄉㄧˋ31頁ㄧㄝˋ喔ㄛ！）

a.) ● ● ● ● ● ● ● ● ● ● ● ● ● ● ● ●

b.) ● ● ● ● ● ● ● ● ● ● ● ● ● ●

c.) ● ● ● ● ● ● ● ● ● ● ● ● ● school

d.) ● ● ● ● ● ● ● ● ● ● ● ● shop

Part. 2

怎ㄗㄣˇ麼˙辦ㄅㄢˋ？賽ㄙㄞˋ皮ㄆㄧˊ和ㄏㄜˊ柔ㄖㄡˊ依一回ㄏㄨㄟˊ家ㄐㄧㄚ途ㄊㄨˊ中ㄓㄨㄥ，遇ㄩˋ到ㄉㄠˋ一一隻ㄓ兇ㄒㄩㄥ狠ㄏㄣˇ的ㄉㄜ˙大ㄉㄚˋ狗ㄍㄡˇ緊ㄐㄧㄣˇ追ㄓㄨㄟ著ㄓㄜ˙他ㄊㄚ們ㄇㄣ˙不ㄅㄨˋ放ㄈㄤˋ！請ㄑㄧㄥˇ你ㄋㄧˇ幫ㄅㄤ助ㄓㄨˋ他ㄊㄚ們ㄇㄣ˙安ㄢ全ㄑㄩㄢˊ的ㄉㄜ˙回ㄏㄨㄟˊ到ㄉㄠˋ家ㄐㄧㄚ吧ㄅㄚ˙！(走ㄗㄡˇ法ㄈㄚˇ：請ㄑㄧㄥˇ從ㄘㄨㄥˊ START 的ㄉㄜ˙地ㄉㄧˋ方ㄈㄤ往ㄨㄤˇ下ㄒㄧㄚˋ走ㄗㄡˇ，遇ㄩˋ到ㄉㄠˋ彎ㄨㄢ要ㄧㄠˋ轉ㄓㄨㄢˇ，但ㄉㄢˋ是ㄕˋ不ㄅㄨˋ能ㄋㄥˊ夠ㄍㄡˋ逆ㄋㄧˋ著ㄓㄜ˙箭ㄐㄧㄢˋ頭ㄊㄡˊ方ㄈㄤ向ㄒㄧㄤˋ走ㄗㄡˇ唷ㄧ！)

（正ㄓㄥˋ確ㄑㄩㄝˋ答ㄉㄚˊ案ㄢˋ在ㄗㄞˋ第ㄉㄧˋ31頁ㄧㄝˋ喔ㄛˊ！）

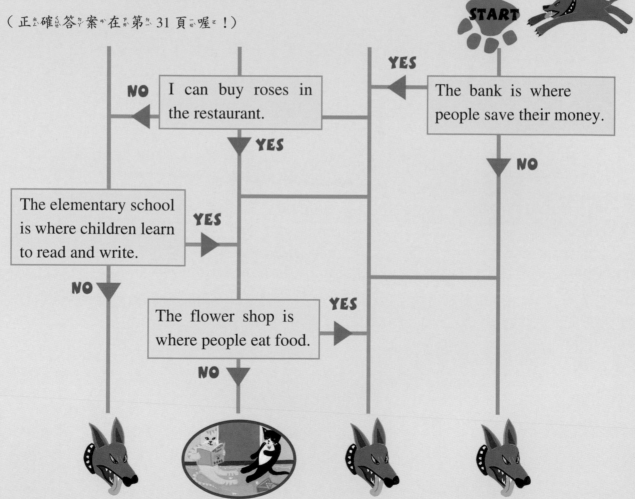

1. a.) bank
    b.) restaurant
    c.) elementary
    d.) flower

2.

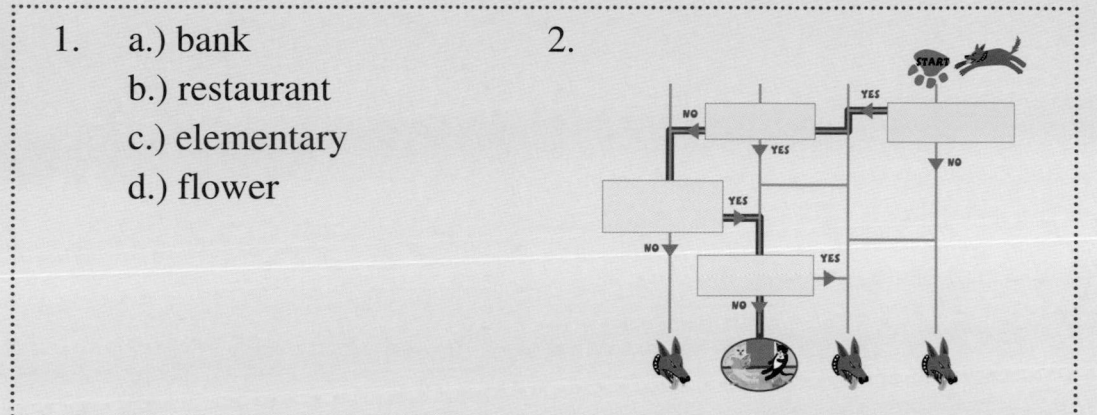

Author's Note

I love to read. Every night before I go to sleep I read. Zippy and Zoe like to sit with me when I read. They try to put their faces up to the book. It looks like they are reading.

作者的話

我喜歡閱讀，每天晚上睡覺前，我都會看書。當我看書的時候，賽皮和柔依喜歡和我坐在一起；他們會試著把臉湊到書前面，看起來就好像他們在讀書一樣。

🐾 About the Author

Carla Golembe is the illustrator of thirteen children's books, five of which she wrote. Carla has won several awards including a New York Times Best Illustrated Picture Book Award. She has also received illustration awards from Parents' Choice and the American Folklore Society. She has twenty-five years of college teaching experience and, for the last thirteen years, has given speaker presentations and workshops to elementary schools. She lives in Southeast Florida, with her husband Joe and her cats Zippy and Zoe.

🐾 關於作者

Carla Golembe 擔任過十三本童書的繪者，其中五本是由她寫作的。Carla 曾多次獲獎，包括《紐約時報》最佳圖畫書獎。她也曾獲全美父母首選基金會，以及美國民俗學會的插畫獎項。她有二十五年的大學教學經驗，而在過去的十三年中，曾經在多所小學中演講及舉辦研討會。她目前和丈夫 Joe 以及她的貓——賽皮與柔依，住在美國佛羅里達州東南部。

賽皮與柔依系列

ZIPPY AND ZOE SERIES

想知道我們發生了什麼驚奇又爆笑的事嗎？
歡迎學習英文0-2年的小朋友一起來分享我們的故事──
「賽皮與柔依系列」，讓你在一連串有趣的事情中學英文！

精裝／附中英雙語朗讀CD／全套六本

Carla Golembe 著／繪
本局編輯部 譯

Hello！我是賽皮，
我喜歡畫畫、做餅乾，還有
跟柔依一起去海邊玩。偷偷
告訴你們一個秘密：我在馬
戲團表演過喔！

Hi，我是柔依，
今年最開心的事，就是賽皮送
我一張他親手畫的生日卡片！
賽皮是我最要好的朋友，他很
聰明也很可愛，我們兩個常常
一起出去玩！

賽皮與柔依系列有：

① 賽皮與綠色顏料
(Zippy and the Green Paint)

② 賽皮與馬戲團
(Zippy and the Circus)

③ 賽皮與超級大餅乾
(Zippy and the Very Big Cookie)

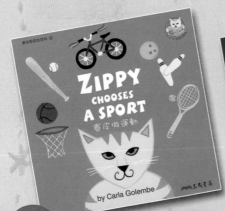

④ 賽皮做運動
(Zippy Chooses a Sport)

⑤ 賽皮學認字
(Zippy Reads)

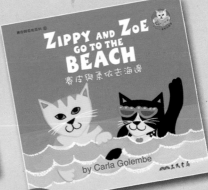

⑥ 賽皮與柔依去海邊
(Zippy and Zoe Go to the Beach)

I Love My Family Series

我愛我的家系列

Kathleen R. Seaton　著／姚紅　繪

附中英雙語朗讀 CD

適讀對象：學習英文 0～2 年者（國小 1～3 年級適讀）

六本全新創作的中英雙語繪本，
六個溫馨幽默的故事，
帶領小朋友們進入單純可愛的小班的生活，
跟他一起分享和家人之間親密的感情！

國家圖書館出版品預行編目資料

Zippy Reads:賽皮學認字 / Carla Golembe著;Carla
Golembe繪;本局編輯部譯.－－初版一刷.－－臺
北市: 三民，2006
　　面；　　公分.－－(Fun心讀雙語叢書.賽皮與柔
依系列)
中英對照
ISBN 957－14－4454－5　（精裝）

1.英國語言－讀本
523.38　　　　　　　　　　　　　　94026568

網路書店位址　http://www.sanmin.com.tw

© 　Zippy Reads
　　──賽皮學認字

著作人　Carla Golembe
繪　者　Carla Golembe
譯　者　本局編輯部
發行人　劉振強
著作財
產權人　三民書局股份有限公司
　　　　臺北市復興北路386號
發行所　三民書局股份有限公司
　　　　地址／臺北市復興北路386號
　　　　電話／(02)25006600
　　　　郵撥／0009998－5
印刷所　三民書局股份有限公司
門市部　復北店／臺北市復興北路386號
　　　　重南店／臺北市重慶南路一段61號
初版一刷　2006年1月
編　號　S 806211
定　價　新臺幣壹佰捌拾元整
行政院新聞局登記證局版臺業字第○二○○號

有著作權‧不准侵害

ISBN　957－14－4454－5　（精裝）